ROCKS IN MY HEAD

Poems for Young People
About Rocks, Minerals, and Crystals

by

Judi A. Rypma

Dear Kathy,
It has been an amazing
experience getting to know you.
All best to you in your
future!

2019

ROCK HOUND PRESS

Text and photos © 2016 Judith A. Rypma
ISBN: 978-0-692-55356-5

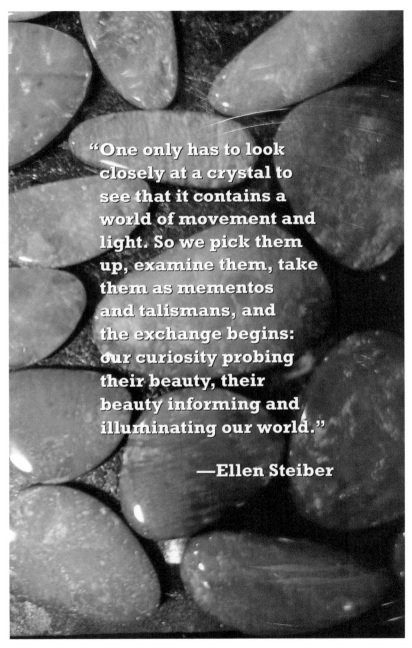

"One only has to look closely at a crystal to see that it contains a world of movement and light. So we pick them up, examine them, take them as mementos and talismans, and the exchange begins: our curiosity probing their beauty, their beauty informing and illuminating our world."

—Ellen Steiber

"Thy mind is very opal."
—Shakespeare

Table of Contents

Tone Deaf 1

When I Close My Eyes 2

Agates 3

70 Percent of Dust Is Quartz 4

Crystal Love 5

Vivianite 6

Amethyst Love 7

The Pearl 8

Rock Shopping 9

Opal Love 10

Sulphur 11

Mineral Power 12

Life of a Pearl 13

Obituary 14

Tanka to the Compass 16

Orange Sense: Sensory Poems 17

Biology 18

Dioptase 19

Cave Tanka 20

Rhodonite 21

Rubies 22

What's Best About Reading 23

Samsonite 24

Baltic Cinquain 25

Parent Rock 26

Collecting. 27

English Homework 28

Gems of the Soil, Gems of the Sky 29

Nature's Fingerprints 30

When I'm Angry 31

From The Kid Who'd Someday Invent

   Synthetic Emeralds 32

"As The Rocks Turn" 34

Subpoena 36

Mother's Earrings 37

Rocks In My Head 38

Recommended Books For New And/Or

   Younger Rock Hounds 41

Recommended For Advanced

   Rock Hounds 43

Web Rocks 45

About The Author: 47

TONE DEAF

They claim
you can recharge crystals
with music

that they're receptive
to sound patterns

prefer tones
of human voices

so I hide mine
in our cement basement

in case my singing
transforms them back
into just plain rocks.

WHEN I CLOSE MY EYES

sometimes I see
swirls of color:
tangerine, lavender, fuchsia

or teal oceans
fruit juice skies
marshmallow clouds—

all swirling
dancing, shifting
twirling

as if just maybe
there are opals
growing in my head.

AGATES

Peacock eyes
lavender laces
iris petticoats
cameo faces

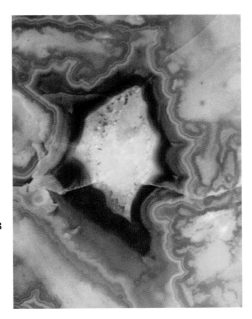

fanciful scallops
concentric rings
fiery bubbles
butterfly wings

feathered plumes
tree trunk bands
mossy branches
milky strands

winding rivers
golden twirls
crystal dancers
onyx swirls.

70 PERCENT OF DUST IS QUARTZ

Now that I know the truth
I cannot clean my room—
not if it means sending
all those rocks to their doom

CRYSTAL LOVE

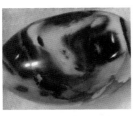

Chrysocolla's vivid faces

Ruby's chromium traces.

Yellow Jasper's tiger shade

Stibnite's silver prism parade.

Turquoise's shade of blue-green

Azurite's metallic sheen.

Labrodorite's blue twinkles

Lapis's golden sprinkles.

Onyx's cameo muse

Vivianite's varied blues

Emerald's fiery hues.

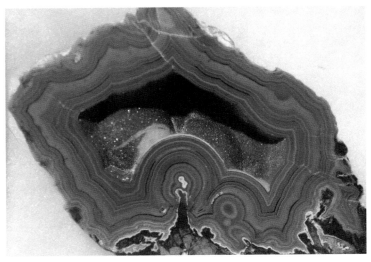

VIVIANITE

Only a secondary mineral
found in tin mines
looking plain, pale
wearing a fan
of flexible
thin white sheets

but pick it up
to provide space, air
and immediately it begins to turn color
**unfolding feathers in vivid
bluish-green hues of a peacock.**

AMETHYST LOVE

Clusters of grape crystals
climb a crystal matrix
darkening as they ripen.
Their sharp edges point
at you as if to say
I'm too cold
to taste
but sweet
to the heart.

THE PEARL

It rocks gently
for years. Snuggles
inside an abalone shell.
Like sleeping on a bed
quilted in rainbows.

ROCK SHOPPING

They're arranged in bins:
polished onyx
agate slices
chunky geodes
amber bubbles
quartz nuggets
aventurine mints

and I can't help
sifting through them
like fingering
all the candies
in a trick-or-treat bag.

OPAL LOVE

Giant jawbreakers
colors of soft soap bubbles
soil's coral reefs.

SULPHUR

It is its own
yellow—not quite
lemon, sunbeam, dandelion
perhaps
Earth's longest blooming
daffodil.

MINERAL POWER

Switch on a light
and electricity surges
through copper wires.
Flows into filament
made from tungsten
extracted from wolframite
so that minerals
light up my world.

LIFE
OF A PEARL

Born from a tiny sand grain,
she clings tightly to her mother, the
oyster. Grows into a beautiful, translucent
gem safe in her rainbow chambers until one
day divers arrive. Yank her from her home. Ship
her far away to a dry place where just maybe
somebody will wear her around a neck. Yet
she will never forget, will always envision
gold, silver, quartz sands, ultramarine
seas, palm trees waving a sad
farewell.

OBITUARY

Separate funerals are being held today
for the Coral family,
all lost at sea
in separate incidents.
Arrangements are pending for

Mrs. Lettuce Coral,
who died of injuries sustained
when two ships ran a reef signal.
An autopsy revealed
Mrs. Coral's head had been split
by a boat's hull
and her limbs scattered
by subsequent propellers.

She was preceded in death
only hours earlier by a loyal husband,
Mr. Elkhorn Coral,
smushed by a snorkeler.

Last year the Corals' son,
Fire Coral, succumbed
to injuries suffered when
a cruise ship anchor
cracked his spine.

The family matriarch,
Bamboo Coral,
died last month at age two thousand—
killed in a dynamite fishing blast.

A memorial has been set up
at Oil Spill Recovery Home.
Contributions for the family
may be made to
www.savethecoralreefs.org.

TANKA TO THE COMPASS

Cubes of magnetite
crystals glittering in ore.
Tiny steel needle
from iron combined with coal
points the way to go.

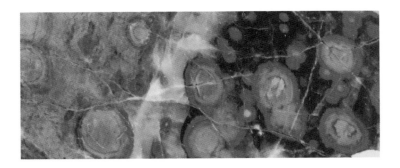

ORANGE SENSE: Sensory Poems

Excitement is poppy jasper.
Sounds like bubbles popping in a lava tube.
Smells like marigolds.
Tastes like orange licorice.
Looks like a monarch butterfly.
Excitement feels like a Halloween costume.

Happiness is spessartine.
Sounds like an oriole's chirp.
Smells like peach sherbet.
Tastes like a honeycomb.
Looks like winking fireflies.
Happiness feels like waving sparklers.

BIOLOGY

I am made of iron
and copper, potassium, zinc
salt, fluorine, iodine—
eighty different minerals

so I carry my rock collection
everywhere I go.
It came free with my body.

DIOPTASE

Too close to the stove
it will dehydrate.
Recipes call it
copper silicate.

Warmed up slightly
it starts to flake.
Turns to black toast
if you try to bake.

Blue and green squeezes
from two frosting tubes
produce hydrous forms
shaped in tiny cubes.

It looks as if each
shade twinkles.
Reminding me
of cupcake sprinkles.

CAVE TANKA

Limestone wears away.
Water continues to drip.
Air fills up the cracks.
Stalagmites widen into
seven-layer wedding cakes.

RHODONITE

Its licorice seas
and raspberry continents
form a new planet.

RUBIES

Touch one to your tongue
and it tastes like red ice
as its thermal conductivity
draws heat from your body.

Peer inside and gaze upon
pagodas, elephants, teak trees
in fiery crimson flames
that instantly rewarm you.

WHAT'S BEST ABOUT READING

Analyzing metaphoric layers

sifting pages for lucid images

panning for flecks of gold.

Even in mines with few nuggets

the real pleasure comes from

examining pebbles—

each streak of color

scattering my brain with gems.

SAMSONITE

At the airport
I watch luggage

bumped, thumped
                    smashed   bashed
       kicked   nicked

crushed   smushed
              smacked   whacked

so why is my suitcase
named after
one of the only rocks
so delicate
it must remain in shade
because even a brief
exposure to light
can destroy it?

BALTIC CINQUAIN

Amber.
Beaded honey.
Angels stitching sunbeams.
My soul unraveling riches.
Spun gold.

PARENT ROCK

My Dad acts as if
he's nephrite: one
of the world's
toughest minerals.

But he's only stern, stony
on the outside. If I tap him
just the right way

he opens up. Reveals
the shimmering goodness
of a crystal geode.

COLLECTING

Museums sell specimens
in tiny plastic cases,
each brilliant chunk
cushioned on foam

so I save up coins
the way a dragon
covets shiny trinkets,
hoards its treasure.

ENGLISH HOMEWORK

It's due tomorrow
so all night
I chisel sentences
reshape paragraphs
buff rough spots
solder split infinitives
retool, buff.

Occasionally I pause,
turn over the assignment
in my head. Same way
a rock tumbler spins stones in a cage.

If only I had a jeweler
to remove imperfections
or a rack of wheels, spheres, cones, needles
to guide changes with a knowledgeable hand.

It's a process like this essay
except I don't have those tiny diamond particles
they press into special polishing powder
to remove flaws and enhance
layers of agate, chalcedony.

Eventually I have to stop
because no engraver can maintain
a high level of precision and skill
for too many consecutive hours

can only hope an intricate cameo
has emerged—delicately carved,
highly crafted piece of writing

my teacher will recognize
as a masterpiece
when she picks up that graphite pencil.

GEMS OF THE SOIL, GEMS OF THE SKY

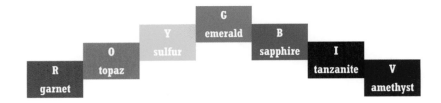

There must be a rainbow growing beneath the earth.

NATURE'S FINGERPRINTS

On the outside
no two exactly alike
though each emerald flashes
all the green nuances
of spring.

Peer inside
to discover a secret
garden. Hope to be
the lucky clover
who finds one.

WHEN I'M ANGRY

I'm an ancient emerald:
pent up pressure
blocked by sedimentary layers

until it surfaces
as all hot air and water
dissipating harmlessly
in the space my family
must share with me.

When I don't know what to do
with rage
that keeps running into
impenetrable shale

I imagine
millions of years passing
until underground pools
develop within. They cool

slowly, peacefully.
Forming lovely crystals
at the edges of my mind.

FROM THE KID WHO'D SOMEDAY INVENT
SYNTHETIC EMERALDS*

Dear Dad,

I'm very, very sorry
for blowing up the house
but after I learned in school
how diamonds are just
a form of graphite
it made perfect sense
to mix it with melted iron
blend the two into liquid nitrogen.

You were really supportive
giving me permission
to use the basement for experiments
so I don't think it's fair now
to tell me to find a new hobby.

Who knows what could happen
if I persevere? I'm still young
but someday I might discover
something even better than
that French scientist's ruby soup.
He kept at it, and eventually
came up with imitation sapphires.
His Dad probably never ordered him
to collect stamps or build ship models.

I don't have millions of years
to wait for precious stones to form
so when you stop hollering
louder than the explosion

I hope you'll still consider me
your gem of a son.

Love,

Carroll Chatham

1935

* In the 1940s, after many, many failed attempts, Carroll
  Chatham developed a method for making synthetic
  emeralds. The largest one he created, now on display at
  the Smithsonian, weighs 1,014 carats. The process takes
  9 months, and Mr. Chatham's son keeps it a secret to this
  day.

"AS THE ROCKS TURN"

My Dear Smoky Quartz:

Stop pretending
you are me
or I may have to sue you
for impersonating an imperial gemstone.

Sincerely,

Topaz

My Dear Topaz:

How can you resent me
when everyone knows
imitation is the sincerest form of flattery?

You come in so many hues
it hardly seems fair
to the rest of us

to deny me the opportunity
to strut my orange fire
or borrow just one
of your sunset colors.

Go ahead, sue me.

I have references. Ask citrine
who doesn't seem to mind
any more than actors do
when Hollywood award shows
hire seat sitters
so the audience looks full.

All I want
is to beautify someone.
After all, kazulite and Sodalite
do it all the time—and Lapis Lazuli
simply puts up with it. Plus

it gives more people the chance
to enjoy our stunning charms
since you and Lapis
have priced yourselves out of the market.

Offended in Switzerland,

Smoky Quartz

Dear Smoky Quartz:

Yes, the world is full of imitators.
However, please keep in mind that falsification
of minerals and crystals is known as FORGERY.
My orange cousin Amber
has multiple charges pending against
the plastics industry. She also told me
about a breach of promise suit
on behalf of all the duped insects
thinking they would live for forty thousand years
in soft comfort, not get dumped at a garage sale.
But I digress.... I DO sympathize, but
you need to get over it.
You're just a lump of quartz
treated with high levels of radiation.
Find a better way to use that energy.

Her Royal Highness,

Topaz

SUBPOENA

In the matter of the Plaintiff, Mr. Smoky Quartz
and all heirs & successors

VS.

Defendant: Ms. Topaz

The defendant is hereby ordered to appear in
court in the matter of unfair trade practices market
monopoly. Until such time as this pending suit
reaches the Supreme Court of Rocks docket, you
are ordered to cease and desist any contact with
the Plaintiff. Additionally, you are ordered to refrain
from misrepresenting yourself as the only "genuine"
and "high quality" orange gem.

Although you are encouraged to secure your own
attorney, this office suggests you save your fees and
refer as precedent to the landmark decision, Jadeite
versus Nephrite.

J. D. Symmetry, Esq.

P.S. On a personal note, I would advise an out-of-
court settlement. I also have been contacted by
someone named Ms. Citrine, who has asked that I
represent her, as well. You may be expensive, but
you have no idea how much I can cost.

MOTHER'S

It's as if she's wearing
the sky—marble clouds
drifting across the same
perfect shade of blue
Michelangelo mixed
to create heaven
in the Sistine's dome.

EARRINGS

A turn of her head
reveals the gold glitter
of pyrite inclusions
that give lapis lazuli
its sparkle. That reflect
stars twinkling above
in my mother's eyes.

37

ROCKS IN MY HEAD

Call it obsessive-compulsive
but I'll never stop collecting them—
not the ones in the soil, caves, rivers
not the ones rolling in my brain.

Sometimes they rattle around
and I imagine a kaleidoscope
with colors tumbling, bits and pieces,
entire patterns emerging

smoother and smoother each year
no two exactly the same
or so I'd like to think.
Can't sell them, though

nor share too many—
not my personal assortment.
Besides, it's not fair
to mine all the gems at once.

Instead I hoard them for times
I might want to read, study, browse
online sites, learn to do something new—
anything to keep my specimens

from getting dusty. Before tests
it seems impossible there are enough
so I take one out and polish it
or even let the shapes and sizes

metamorphose into something else.
Sometimes I find things up there
I didn't know existed—like all
the new species geologists discover

and I look forward to rock hunting
for the rest of my life. Know I'll keep
finding more gifts from the earth,
hope I'll keep mining those in my head.

RECOMMENDED BOOKS FOR NEW and/or YOUNGER ROCK HOUNDS

Barnes-Svarney, Patricia L. *Born of Heat and Pressure: Mountains and Metamorphic Rocks.* NJ: Enslow Publishers, Inc., 1991.

Busbey III, Arthur B. et al. *Rocks & Fossils.* San Francisco: Fog City Press, Rev. 2007.

Cheney, Glenn Alan. *Mineral Resources.* NY: Franklin Watts, 1985.

Claybourne, Anna. *Rocks and Minerals.* Illus. Michael Posen. Bath, UK: Parragon Publishing, 2001.

Dineem, Jacqueline. *Metals and Minerals.* NJ: Enslow Publishers, Inc., 1988.

Gans, Roma. *Let's Go Rock Collecting.* Illus. Holly Keller. NY: HarperCollins, 1997.

_____. *Rock Collecting.* Illus. Holly Keller. NY: HarperCollins Publishers, 1984.

Hoban, Tana. *Animal, Vegetable, or Mineral?* NY: Greenwillow Books, 1995.

Hunt, Joyce and Millicent E. Selsam. *A First Look at Rocks.* Illus. Harriett Springer. NY: Walker & Co., 1984.

Kerrod, Robin. *The World's Mineral Resources.* NY: Thomson Learning, 1994.

Kittinger, Jo S. *A Look at Rocks: From Coal to Kimberlite.* NY: Franklin Watts, 1997.

Morris, Neil. *Rocks & Minerals.* NY: Crabtree Publishing, 1998.

Olson, Donald. *Earth's Treasures (Eyes on Adventure).* Kidsbooks, 2007.

Parker, Steve. *Eyewitness Explorer's Rocks and Minerals.* London: Dorling Kindersley, 1993.

Pellant, Chris and Helen. *1000 Facts on Rocks & Minerals.* NY: Barnes & Noble, 2006. (orig 2005 by Miles Kelly Publishing Ltd.)

Pellant, Chris. *Rocks and Fossils.* Boston: Kingfisher, Houghton Mifflin, 2003.

Pough, Frederick H. Peterson. *First Guide to Rocks and Minerals: A simplified field guide to common gems, ores, and other rocks and minerals.* Boston: Houghton Mifflin Co., 1991.

Symes, Dr. R. F. and Dr. R. R. Harding. *Eyewitness Books: Crystal & Gem.* NY: DK Publishing, 2004.

Symes, Dr. R. F. and the staff of the Natural History Museum of London. *Eyewitness Books: Rocks and Minerals.* NY: Alfred A. Knopf, Dorling Kindersley,1988.

RECOMMENDED FOR ADVANCED ROCK HOUNDS
(most of which I consulted when writing my own poems)

Brocardo, G. *Minerals & Gemstones of the World: A NatureTrek Guide.* Trans. Dr. Lucia Woodward. Ed. David A. Smith. Brunel House. England: David & Charles, 1994.

Busbey, Arthur B. et al. *Rocks & Fossils.* San Francisco: Fog City Press 1996. Revised 2007.

Cipriani, Curzio and Alessandro Borelli. *Simon & Schuster's Guide to Gems and Precious Stones.* Trans. Valerie Palmer. Ed. Kennie Lyman. NY: Fireside Book, 1986.

Farndon, John. *The Complete Guide to Rocks & Minerals.* London: Hermes House, 2006.

Finlay, Victoria. *Jewels: A Secret History.* NY: Ballantine Books, 2006.

Guastoni, Alessandro and Roberto Appiani. *Minerals.* Trans. Jay Hyams. Buffalo, NY: Firefly Books, 2005.

Hochleitner, Rupert. *Minerals: Identifying, Classifying, and Collecting Them.* Trans. Kathleen Luft. 1st English language ed. Hauppauge, NY: Barron's Educational Series, Inc., 1994.

Kouřimský, Dr. Jiří. Ed. Randolph Lucas. *The Illustrated Encyclopedia of Minerals & Rocks.* Trans. Vera Gissing. Secaucus, NJ: Chartwell Books Inc, 1993.

Lagomarsino, James. *A Pocket Guide to Rocks & Minerals.* Bath, UK: Parragon Books, 2008.

O'Donoghue, Michael. *The Pocket Guide to Rocks and Minerals.* London: Parkgate Books Ltd., 1999. Reprinted from 1991.

Schumann, Walter. *Gemstones of the World.* Trans. Annette and Daniel Shea. 3rd ed. NY: Sterling Publishing, Inc., 2006.

Thomas, Arthur. *The Gemstones Handbook: Properties, Identification, and Use.* NY: Fall River Press, 2008.

Walters, Raymond J. L. *The Power of Gemstones.* Carlton Books, Ltd., 1996.

WEB ROCKS

If you'd like to find pictures of some of the rocks
mentioned in my poems or just learn more about
rocks, minerals, and crystals, check out some of the
excellent and helpful websites listed below:

Bill Nye the Science Guy
http://nyelabs.kcts.org/

Bob's Rock Shop
http://www.rockhounds.com/

Field Museum of Natural History of Chicago
http://www.fmnh.org/

Geoprime Minerals & Earth Materials Company,
http://www.geoprime.com/mineral/

Irving Family Web Pages: Rock Collecting
http://www.irving.org/rocks

The Mineral Gallery
http://mineral.galleries.com/default.htm

Minerals by Name
**http://www.galleries.com/mineral/by_name.
htm**

Smithsonian Gem & Mineral Collection
**http://galaxy.einet.net/images/gem/gems-
icons.htm/#COPYRIGHT**

ABOUT THE AUTHOR:

Judi A. Rypma started collecting rocks at age 5.
"My mother used to take me to the public museum
when I was in grade school. It was there—and
walking home from school along railroad tracks and
through a gravel pit—that I fell in love with rocks."

Ms. Rypma has published several adult collections
of poems, many of which feature rock and gem
metaphors. She teaches Children's & Adolescent
Literature at Western Michigan University.